30 DAY MIND-BODY-SOUL
DEVOTIONAL

STANDING STRONG
Arise and Awaken

CATALINA   PEREZ

COPYRIGHT

TABLE OF CONTENTS

ACKNOWLEDGEMENTS

First, I want to glorify my father and give him all the thanks and praise. With him I have continue to breathe and live

I want to thank my children Sade & Nathan for trusting the process and walking this out with me.

Pastor Doraine Parker- Mother, Leader, and Woman of God I thank you for your obedience in the 8 am prayers and speaking life into me

Vision Coach Kim Springer, I thank you for your daily commitment to rewire my brain to the already DONE place.

Apostle Tanya, I thank you for allowing me to discover some of my hidden talents and for your overall support

I want to thank all the women I have connected with on this journey of self-love and discovery.

I want to thank all the intercessors who prayed for this moment

Last but most importantly, I want to give thanks to my mother Catalina Soto Mar who has always believed and supported me, reminding me of all my potential

THE AGREEMENT

STANDING STRONG
Arise and Awaken

I resolve to put the Word before the world, because I believe Jesus Christ is worthy of my first, best and last moments. He is the ONE... and I am honored and filled with JOY knowing I am his DAUGHTER and DISCIPLE as I daily come to him and give thanks for his mercy and grace.

I will abide in God's love by believing in HIS unconditional love for me and loving others in the same way. I will LOVE like he LOVES me.
I will be a doer of God's word, and not a hearer only, so that I will not deceive myself

I believe the time I spend with Jesus is priceless, its perspective shifting, mindset shifting, direction giving and I will SHOUT and SING to the heavens as I preach the Gospel to my heart daily.
I pick up my spiritual fork and nourish my soul with the Word of Truth and when I don't feel like picking up my Bible or praying, I will do it anyway because I know that he fuels my hunger.

I resolve to do this, not on my own efforts but by his might and power at work within me. By his grace, I will CHOOSE the better portion that will last forever, keeping my eyes fixed on Jesus and my heart set on eternity.

Name   **Date**

What is your WHY?
(Take a few minutes to sit and ponder that thought)
really sit with it... (This is your time for YOU)

_____

_____

_____

_____

_____

_____

_____

_____

_____

_____

_____

_____

_____

_____

_____

_____

_____

_____

_____

_____

_____

It is the foundation YOU will need to motivate yourself to staying committed to making lasting changes.

DAY 1

Scripture:

Have I not commanded you? Be strong and courageous do not be afraid; your God will be with you wherever you go.

Joshua 1:9

Who are you? What do you love about yourself?

_____
_____
_____
_____
_____
_____
_____
_____
_____
_____
_____
_____
_____
_____
_____
_____
_____
_____
_____
_____
_____
_____
_____
_____
_____
_____
_____
_____
_____
_____
_____

Write the Activation

Activation: I AM much-loved Child of God and no matter the circumstances I will OVERCOME!!

_____
_____
_____
_____
_____
_____
_____
_____
_____
_____
_____
_____
_____
_____
_____
_____
_____
_____
_____
_____
_____
_____
_____
_____
_____
_____
_____
_____
_____
_____
_____
_____
_____

BE STRONG AND COURAGEOUS JOSHUA 1:9

DAY 2

Scripture:

Therefore, I urge you, brothers, and sisters, in view of god's mercy to offer your bodies as a living sacrifice, holy and pleasing to god - this is your true and proper worship.

Romans 12:1

What do I need to believe and who do I need to become in, order to live
a life of prosperity?

_____

_____

_____

_____

_____

_____

_____

_____

_____

_____

_____

_____

_____

_____

_____

_____

_____

_____

_____

_____

_____

_____

_____

_____

_____

_____

Write the Activation

Activation: It is working! God who began the good work in me is working to this day. As it works IN it will work OUT!!

_____

_____

_____

_____

_____

_____

_____

_____

_____

_____

_____

_____

_____

_____

_____

_____

_____

_____

_____

_____

_____

_____

_____

YOUR WORD
IS A LAMP
TO MY FEET AND
A LIGHT TO
MY PATH
PSALM 119:105

DAY 3

Scripture:

Now faith is the assurance of things hoped for the conviction of things not seen.

Hebrews 11:1

If I knew I was safe and fully supported what would I create in my business this year?

_____

_____

_____

_____

_____

_____

_____

_____

_____

_____

_____

_____

_____

_____

_____

_____

_____

_____

_____

_____

_____

_____

_____

_____

_____

_____

_____

Write the Activation

Activation: I am outgrowing this place as I become who I am already in Christ.

_____
_____
_____
_____
_____
_____
_____
_____
_____
_____
_____
_____
_____
_____
_____
_____
_____
_____
_____
_____
_____
_____
_____

I CAN DO ALL THINGS THROUGH CHRIST WHO STRENGTHENS ME PHILLIPIANS 4:13

DAY 4

Scripture:

You will keep in perfect peace those whose minds are steadfast, because they trust in you.

Isaiah 26:3

What area in your life is God asking you to surrender?

_____

_____

_____

_____

_____

_____

_____

_____

_____

_____

_____

_____

_____

_____

_____

_____

_____

_____

_____

_____

_____

_____

_____

_____

_____

_____

_____

_____

Write the Activation

Activation: I have a mental toughness & mental enoughness to rest in God's plan for my life.

REPEAT OUT LOUD:
We're moving mountains this YEAR!
UNAFRAID!!

REPEAT OUT LOUD:
We're moving mountains this YEAR!
UNAFRAID!!

REPEAT OUT LOUD:
We're moving mountains this YEAR!
UNAFRAID!!

FOR WITH GOD NOTHING SHALL BE IMPOSSIBLE LUKE 1:37

DAY 5

Scripture:

If we are faithless, he remains faithful for he cannot disown himself

2 Timothy 2:13

What are some things that God has brought you out of?

_____

_____

_____

_____

_____

_____

_____

_____

_____

_____

_____

_____

_____

_____

_____

_____

_____

_____

_____

_____

_____

_____

_____

_____

_____

_____

Write the Activation

Activation: Yes, I am worthy; worthy of my desires

BLESSED ARE THE PURE IN HEART; FOR THEY SHALL SEE GOD MATTHEW 5:8

DAY 6

Scripture:

When Jacob awoke from his sleep, he thought, "Surely the Lord is in this place, and I was not aware of it.

Acts 1:8

What do I hope to learn through this month? What steps have I taken to prepare for what's ahead?

_____

_____

_____

_____

_____

_____

_____

_____

_____

_____

_____

_____

_____

_____

_____

_____

_____

_____

_____

_____

_____

_____

_____

_____

_____

_____

_____

Write the Activation

Activation: Goodness is assigned to me whether I'm on a bus that's serving me or not

HAVING HOPE WILL GIVE YOU COURAGE

JOB 11:18

DAY 7

Scripture:

May he give you the desire of your heart and make all your plans succeed.

Psalm 20:4

What truly matters to your heart? And are you giving it sufficient time for daily nourishment?

_____
_____
_____
_____
_____
_____
_____
_____
_____
_____
_____
_____
_____
_____
_____
_____
_____
_____
_____
_____
_____
_____
_____
_____
_____
_____

Write the Activation

Activation: Unplanned or intimidating circumstances are not a threat to my vision. It is happening this circumstance to PROPEL me.

_____

_____

_____

_____

_____

_____

_____

_____

_____

_____

_____

_____

_____

_____

_____

_____

_____

_____

_____

_____

_____

_____

_____

_____

_____

WATCH THESE VIDEOS:

Restoring Your Mind| Steven Furtick
https://www.youtube.com/watch?v=MwOlq-gR3vU

Michael Todd: Your Pain Prepares You for Your Purpose
https://youtu.be/8MWLFnw6bw4

WORSHIP TIME:

Jireh | Elevation Worship & Maverick City

https://youtu.be/mC-zw0zCCtg

Raise A Hallelujah (Lyrics) ~ Bethel Music

https://youtu.be/e3RRU25dpPg

Nothing Else (feat. Cody Carnes) // The Belonging Co
https://youtu.be/DLBvCTV23qw

FOR WHERE YOUR TREASURE IS, THERE YOUR HEART WILL BE ALSO MATTHEW 6:21

DAY 8

Scripture:

Who, being in very nature God, did not consider equality with God something to be used to his own advantage; rather, he made himself nothing by taking the very nature of a servant, being made in human likeness.

Philippians 2: 5-7

What excuses or lies have you told yourself or believed that has stopped you from your purpose?

_____
_____
_____
_____
_____
_____
_____
_____
_____
_____
_____
_____
_____
_____
_____
_____
_____
_____
_____
_____
_____
_____
_____
_____

Write the Activation

Activation: When I was born, I was already rich & wealthy. When I was born, I was already rich & wealthy

I AM FEARFULLY AND WONDERFULLY MADE. PSALM 139:14

DAY 9

Scripture:

You did not choose me, but I chose you and appointed you that you should go and bear fruit and that your fruit should abide, so that whatever you ask the father in my name, he may give it to you.

John 15:16

What will you choose to do for yourself today?

_____

_____

_____

_____

_____

_____

_____

_____

_____

_____

_____

_____

_____

_____

_____

_____

_____

_____

_____

_____

_____

_____

_____

_____

_____

_____

Write the Activation

Activation: I have a Divine processor that searches all things, and he tells me where the GOLD is in my life! Downloading NOW!!

_____

_____

_____

_____

_____

_____

_____

_____

_____

_____

_____

_____

_____

_____

_____

_____

_____

_____

_____

_____

_____

_____

_____

_____

_____

_____

GOD IS WITHIN HER, SHE SHALL NOT FAIL PSALM 46:5

DAY 10

Scripture:

Bear with each other and forgive one another if any of you has a grievance against someone. Forgive as the Lord forgave you.

Colossians 3:13

What does wellness & forgiveness have to do with each other?

Write the Activation

Activation: It is impossible for my beloved to ever call me out HE only calls me up always and forever.

_____

_____

_____

_____

_____

_____

_____

_____

_____

_____

_____

_____

_____

_____

_____

_____

_____

_____

_____

_____

_____

_____

_____

_____

_____

_____

FOR WE WALK BY FAITH NOT BY SIGHT

2 CORINTHIANS 5:7

DAY 11

Scripture:

In his defense Jesus said to them, "My Father is always at his work to this very day, and I too am working."

John 5:17

What is holding you back from the assignment God has given you? Why are you allowing that to hold you back?

_____

_____

_____

_____

_____

_____

_____

_____

_____

_____

_____

_____

_____

_____

_____

_____

_____

_____

_____

_____

_____

_____

_____

_____

_____

Write the Activation

Activation: God's been busy working for me I need to rest to take it all in and trust that he has worked it all out for me.

_____
_____
_____
_____
_____
_____
_____
_____
_____
_____
_____
_____
_____
_____
_____
_____
_____
_____
_____
_____
_____
_____
_____
_____
_____

COMMIT TO THE

LORD

WHATEVER YOU DO,

AND YOUR

PLANS WILL SUCCEED

PROVERBS 16:3

DAY 12

Scripture:

What you decide on will be done, and light will shine on your ways.

Job 22:28

How can you live your life to represent him daily?

_____

_____

_____

_____

_____

_____

_____

_____

_____

_____

_____

_____

_____

_____

_____

_____

_____

_____

_____

_____

_____

_____

_____

_____

_____

_____

_____

_____

_____

Write the Activation

Activation: I'm Coming Out! I am no longer available to create the result I no longer want. From here on out I am employed by my father.

_____

_____

_____

_____

_____

_____

_____

_____

_____

_____

_____

_____

_____

_____

_____

_____

_____

_____

_____

_____

_____

_____

_____

_____

_____

Soak for 5-7 minutes worshipping

Here's a link:

https://youtu.be/CqybaIesbuA

Find a comfortable space and allow your mind to relax as you breathe and start to zone out the noise

Inhale 4 times: God loves me

Exhale 4 times: unconditionally

If you find your mind wondering come back to your breathing and allow his love to rain over, you…

YOU ARE LOVED!!

I AM WITH YOU ALWAYS MATTHEW 28:20

DAY 13

Scripture:

The Lord will vindicate me; your love, Lord, endures forever — do not abandon the works of your hands.

Psalm 138:8

Who do you need to forgive? Do you know why forgiving benefits you? I know it hurts but he's working with you on this. You are not alone.

_____

_____

_____

_____

_____

_____

_____

_____

_____

_____

_____

_____

_____

_____

_____

_____

_____

_____

_____

_____

_____

_____

_____

_____

_____

_____

_____

Write the Activation

Activation: If I'm concerned about it! God is too. If it's on God's mind it's handled!!

ACT JUSTLY,
LOVE MERCY,
WALK HUMBLY.
MICAH 6:8

DAY 14

Scripture:

Therefore, I urge you, brothers, and sisters, in view of God's mercy, to offer your bodies as a living sacrifice, holy and pleasing to God—this is your true and proper worship. Do not conform to the pattern of this world but be transformed by the renewing of your mind. Then you will be able to test and approve what God's will is—his good, pleasing, and perfect will.

Romans 12:1-2

Take time to write down and thank the Father for all he's done!!!

Write the Activation

Activation: I get to choose the vibrations I put in my body, and I choose to rock it out with my team!!

BE STILL
AND KNOW
THAT
I AM GOD
PSALM 46:10

DAY 15

Scripture:

Fill my heart with joy when their grain and new wine abound.

Psalm 4:7

Pick a verse from Proverbs, why did you pick that verse and how did it speak to you?

_____
_____
_____
_____
_____
_____
_____
_____
_____
_____
_____
_____
_____
_____
_____
_____
_____
_____
_____
_____
_____
_____
_____
_____
_____
_____
_____

Write the Activation

Activation: You have put more JOY in my heart like a reservoir. I don't need a cup I just need to DIVE IN!!

_____

_____

_____

_____

_____

_____

_____

_____

_____

_____

_____

_____

_____

_____

_____

_____

_____

_____

_____

_____

_____

_____

_____

_____

LET ALL THAT YOU DO BE DONE IN LOVE

1 CORINTHIANS 16:14

DAY 16

Scripture:

But thanks be to God! He gives us the victory through our Lord Jesus Christ.

1 Corinthians 15:57

What are some areas in your life where you have seen victory and areas where you have experience trials?

_____

_____

_____

_____

_____

_____

_____

_____

_____

_____

_____

_____

_____

_____

_____

_____

_____

_____

_____

_____

_____

_____

_____

_____

_____

_____

_____

_____

_____

Write the Activation

Activation: From where I stand, I see my Victory and the enemy's defeat! Celebrating for the parade of our lives!!

_____

_____

_____

_____

_____

_____

_____

_____

_____

_____

_____

_____

_____

_____

_____

_____

_____

_____

_____

_____

_____

_____

_____

_____

_____

THE LORD IS NEAR TO ALL WHO CALL HIM

PSALM 145:18

DAY 17

Scripture:

May the God of hope fill you with all joy and peace as you trust in him, so that you may overflow with hope by the power of the Holy Spirit.

Roman 15:13

Who has been on your heart recently & how can you go love them like Jesus?

_____
_____
_____
_____
_____
_____
_____
_____
_____
_____
_____
_____
_____
_____
_____
_____
_____
_____
_____
_____
_____
_____
_____
_____
_____
_____

Write the Activation

Activation: Give me 10 Seconds & I'm changing this environment!! 10, 9, 8 Oh Wait! The enemy has already scattered!!

_____

_____

_____

_____

_____

_____

_____

_____

_____

_____

_____

_____

_____

_____

_____

_____

_____

_____

_____

_____

_____

_____

_____

_____

_____

FOR THE WORD OF
THE LORD IS
RIGHT AND TRUE;
HE IS FAITHFUL
IN ALL HE DOES
PSALM 33:4

DAY 18

Scripture:

I will instruct you and teach you in the way you should go; I will counsel you with my loving eye on you.

Psalms 32:8

How is your Soul today?

Circle the ones you relate to at this moment!

Thankful   Pure   Gentle

Strong   Loved   Calm

Grateful   Whole   Hungry

Brave   Peace   Guilty   Busy

Worried   Adventurous   Confident

Restless   Great   Steadfast

I will love myself and I will

Do something for ME!!

(Write down what it means to you to soul care?)

_____
_____
_____
_____
_____
_____
_____
_____
_____
_____
_____
_____
_____
_____
_____
_____

Write the Activation

Activation: I own the meaning of my days and I make them mean that God is still on the dance floor of my heart

_____

_____

_____

_____

_____

_____

_____

_____

_____

_____

_____

_____

_____

_____

_____

_____

_____

_____

_____

_____

_____

_____

_____

_____

_____

BE TRULY GLAD THERE IS WONDERFUL JOY AHEAD 1 PETER 1:6

DAY 19

Scripture:

Through whom we have gained access by faith into this grace in which we now stand. And we boast in the hope of the glory of God.

Romans 5:2

I AM (fill it in)

Write the Activation

Activation: I align my conversation with what Heaven is saying about me.

_____

_____

_____

_____

_____

_____

_____

_____

_____

_____

_____

_____

_____

_____

_____

_____

_____

_____

_____

_____

_____

_____

_____

AFFIRMATIONS

I WILL LET GO OF HOW I THINK TODAY IS
SUPPOSED TO GO AND ACCEPT HOW IT
IMPERFECTLY HAPPENS

I RELEASE PAST VERSIONS OF MYSELF THAT NO
LONGER REFLECT WHO I AM

I APPRECIATE WHO I AM TODAY

I AM CONFIDENT

I AM IN CONTROL OF MY THOUGHTS

I AM LOVED

I AM PEACE

I AM ME

WITH GOD ALL THINGS ARE POSSIBLE

MATTHEW 19:26

DAY 20

Scripture:

Have faith in God, Jesus answered. Truly, I tell you, if anyone says to this mountain, "Go, throw yourself into the sea and does not doubt in their heart but believes that what they say will happen, it will be done for them.

Mark 11:22-23

You are in your dream location. Describe how you feel? What is it like? (Write down the feelings and things you are doing in the "already done" place)

_____

_____

_____

_____

_____

_____

_____

_____

_____

_____

_____

_____

_____

_____

_____

_____

_____

_____

_____

_____

_____

_____

_____

_____

_____

_____

_____

_____

_____

Write the Activation

Activation: I know what to believe to Quantum Leap

_____

_____

_____

_____

_____

_____

_____

_____

_____

_____

_____

_____

_____

_____

_____

_____

_____

_____

_____

_____

_____

_____

_____

_____

_____

CREATE IN ME A PURE HEART, O GOD, AND RENEW A STEADFAST SPIRIT WITHIN ME

PSALM 51:10

DAY 21

Scripture:

Then he said to her, "Daughter, your faith has healed you. Go in peace."

Luke 8:48

So now, that you have wrote down how you feel at that already "Done" place what can you do today to lead you closer to your dreams?

_____

_____

_____

_____

_____

_____

_____

_____

_____

_____

_____

_____

_____

_____

_____

_____

_____

_____

_____

_____

_____

_____

_____

_____

_____

Write the Activation

Activation: If it touches me, it blesses me. If it stings, I can sing!!

_____
_____
_____
_____
_____
_____
_____
_____
_____
_____
_____
_____
_____
_____
_____
_____
_____
_____
_____
_____
_____
_____
_____
_____
_____
_____
_____

IF GOD IS FOR US, WHO CAN BE AGAINST US?

ROMANS 8:31

DAY 22

Scripture:

You see that his faith and his actions were working together, and his faith was made complete by what he did.

James 2:22

What skills and talents are you spiritually blessed with? If you are not sure, sit with The Lord, and ask him to reveal to you.

_____

_____

_____

_____

_____

_____

_____

_____

_____

_____

_____

_____

_____

_____

_____

_____

_____

_____

_____

_____

_____

_____

_____

_____

Write the Activation

Activation: Reach BEYOND where you are

_____

_____

_____

_____

_____

_____

_____

_____

_____

_____

_____

_____

_____

_____

_____

_____

_____

_____

_____

_____

_____

_____

_____

_____

_____

_____

_____

_____

KNOW WHERE YOU
ARE HEADED, AND
YOU WILL
STAY ON
SOLID GROUND
PROVERBS 4:26

DAY 23

Scripture:

May the God of hope fill you with all joy and peace as you trust in him, so that you may overflow with hope by the power of the Holy Spirit.

Romans: 15:13

Stepping into the purpose he has for you. How are you showing up today?

_____

_____

_____

_____

_____

_____

_____

_____

_____

_____

_____

_____

_____

_____

_____

_____

_____

_____

_____

_____

_____

_____

_____

_____

_____

_____

_____

_____

Write the Activation

Activation: God is with me to Master my emotions

_____
_____
_____
_____
_____
_____
_____
_____
_____
_____
_____
_____
_____
_____
_____
_____
_____
_____
_____
_____
_____
_____
_____
_____
_____
_____
_____

WHERE YOU GO I WILL GO, AND WHERE YOU STAY I WILL STAY

RUTH 1:16

DAY 24

Scripture:

This is how we know that we belong to the truth and how we set our hearts at rest in his presence.

1 John 3:19

What steps will you take to strengthen your relationship with Christ?

_____

_____

_____

_____

_____

_____

_____

_____

_____

_____

_____

_____

_____

_____

_____

_____

_____

_____

_____

_____

_____

_____

_____

_____

_____

_____

_____

_____

_____

Write the Activation

Activation: Heaven's exchange department is always open! And I'm good for an exchange today. I receive God's truth for the lie! Oh!! It's a good day!!

_____
_____
_____
_____
_____
_____
_____
_____
_____
_____
_____
_____
_____
_____
_____
_____
_____
_____
_____
_____
_____
_____
_____
_____
_____

MY BELOVED SPOKE
AND SAID
TO ME,
"ARISE, MY DARLING,
MY BEAUTIFUL ONE,
COME WITH ME."
SONG OF SOLOMON 2:10

Soak for 5-7 minutes worshipping

Here's a link
https://youtu.be/amykXSyOG4o

Find a comfortable space and allow your mind to relax as you breathe and start to zone out the noise and distractions

Inhale 4 times: I AM LOVED

Exhale 4 times: By God himself

If you find your mind wondering come back to your breathing and allow his love to rain upon you....

MY SOUL, FIND REST
IN GOD;
MY HOPE
COMES
FROM HIM.
PSALM 62:5

DAY 25

Scripture:

Thou wilt shew me the path of life: in thy presence is fullness of joy; at thy right hand there are pleasures for evermore.

Psalms 16:11

What will I choose to believe today? Are the thoughts impacting me towards a positive way? Or negative way? Am I feeling good? Or am I feeling like I need a push today?

_____

_____

_____

_____

_____

_____

_____

_____

_____

_____

_____

_____

_____

_____

_____

_____

_____

_____

_____

_____

_____

_____

_____

_____

_____

_____

Write the Activation

Activation: I will rejoice in the Lord I feel like doing it again and again and again.

_____

_____

_____

_____

_____

_____

_____

_____

_____

_____

_____

_____

_____

_____

_____

_____

_____

_____

_____

_____

_____

_____

_____

_____

_____

_____

_____

_____

LET YOUR LIGHT SHINE BEFORE OTHERS MATTHEW 5:16

DAY 26

Scripture:

Yet this I call to mind and therefore I have hope: Because of the LORD's great love we are not consumed for his compassions never fail.

Lamentation 3:21-22

How will you let your light shine today? And what will you exhale and let go?

_____

_____

_____

_____

_____

_____

_____

_____

_____

_____

_____

_____

_____

_____

_____

_____

_____

_____

_____

_____

_____

_____

_____

_____

_____

Write the Activation

Activation: It is written! These words are faithful & true. I am NEW around here!

_____

_____

_____

_____

_____

_____

_____

_____

_____

_____

_____

_____

_____

_____

_____

_____

_____

_____

_____

_____

_____

_____

_____

_____

_____

"I KNOW THE PLANS

I HAVE FOR YOU,"

DECLARES

THE LORD, "PLANS

TO GIVE YOU

HOPE."

JEREMIAH 29:11

DAY 27

Scripture:

No temptation has overtaken you except what is common to mankind. And God is faithful; he will not let you be tempted beyond what you can bear. But when you are tempted, he will also provide a way out so that you can endure it.

1 Corinthians 10:13

What is my soul whispering to me, quietly guiding me to understand or act on?

_____
_____
_____
_____
_____
_____
_____
_____
_____
_____
_____
_____
_____
_____
_____
_____
_____
_____
_____
_____
_____
_____
_____
_____
_____
_____
_____
_____

Write the Activation

Activation: As he is, so I am in this World. I LOVE how that sounds!!

_____
_____
_____
_____
_____
_____
_____
_____
_____
_____
_____
_____
_____
_____
_____
_____
_____
_____
_____
_____
_____
_____
_____
_____
_____
_____
_____

GIVE THANKS TO THE LORD, FOR HE IS GOOD; HIS LOVE ENDURES FOREVER.

1 CHRONICLES 16:34

DAY 28

Scripture:

"Forget the former things; do not dwell on the past. See, I am doing a new thing! Now it springs up; do you not perceive it? I am making a way in the wilderness and streams in the wasteland.

Isaiah 43:18-19

Reflect on 10 key points that you came across while working through this book. How will you apply these to your life?

_____
_____
_____
_____
_____
_____
_____
_____
_____
_____
_____
_____
_____
_____
_____
_____
_____
_____
_____
_____
_____
_____
_____
_____
_____
_____
_____
_____
_____

Write the Activation

Activation: I use to be that way. I am not what I use to be. I am BECOMING who already AM. I am HER Now!!!

_____
_____
_____
_____
_____
_____
_____
_____
_____
_____
_____
_____
_____
_____
_____
_____
_____
_____
_____
_____
_____
_____
_____
_____
_____

NEVER WILL
I LEAVE YOU;
NEVER WILL I
FORSAKE
YOU!!
HEBREWS 13:5

DAY 29

Scripture:

Trust in the Lord with all your heart, and do not lean on your own understanding.

Proverbs 3:5

When was the last time you did something that brought you joy? Find time to do something that brings JOY!! What does JOY mean to you?

_____
_____
_____
_____
_____
_____
_____
_____
_____
_____
_____
_____
_____
_____
_____
_____
_____
_____
_____
_____
_____
_____
_____
_____
_____
_____

Write the Activation

Activation: God is with me with me! Ain't no stopping me now. I'm on the MOVE.

_____
_____
_____
_____
_____
_____
_____
_____
_____
_____
_____
_____
_____
_____
_____
_____
_____
_____
_____
_____
_____
_____
_____
_____
_____
_____
_____

BE TRULY GLAD

THERE IS

WONDERFUL

JOY AHEAD

1 PETER 11:6

DAY 30

Scripture:

Consider it pure joy, my brothers, and sisters, whenever you face trials of many kinds, because you know that the testing of your faith produces perseverance.

James 1 2-4

List your wins for the month? (Example: My win was having a deep conversation with a friend) (Having dinner with all your children) Remember all small wins need to be CELEBRATED!!

_____

_____

_____

_____

_____

_____

_____

_____

_____

_____

_____

_____

_____

_____

_____

_____

_____

_____

_____

_____

_____

_____

_____

_____

_____

_____

_____

Write the Activation

Activation: You have put more JOY in my heart like a reservoir. I don't need a cup I just need to DIVE IN!!

_____

_____

_____

_____

_____

_____

_____

_____

_____

_____

_____

_____

_____

_____

_____

_____

_____

_____

_____

_____

_____

_____

_____

_____

_____

_____

_____

_____

_____

LET ALL THAT YOU DO BE DONE IN LOVE.

1 CORINTHIANS 16:14

Join our community by finding me on Facebook:
https://www.facebook.com/groups/730589351032179/

Share your journey by using hashtag
#ariseandawakenwithin

CPSIA information can be obtained
at www.ICGtesting.com
Printed in the USA
BVHW010758040122
625437BV00012B/266